80 001 990 702

KT-371-086

ANCIENT EGYPT
FARMING & FOOD

JANE SHUTER

Heinemann
LIBRARY

First published in Great Britain by Heinemann Library
Halley Court, Jordan Hill, Oxford OX2 8EJ
a division of Reed Educational and Professional Publishing Ltd.
Heinemann is a registered trademark of Reed Educational & Professional Publishing Limited.

OXFORD MELBOURNE AUCKLAND KUALA LUMPUR
SINGAPORE IBADAN NAIROBI KAMPALA
JOHANNESBURG GABORONE PORTSMOUTH NH CHICAGO

© Reed Educational and Professional Publishing Ltd 1999
The moral right of the proprietor has been asserted.

All rights reserved. No part of this publication may be reproduced, stored in a retrieval system, or transmitted in any form or by any means, electronic, mechanical, photocopying, recording, or otherwise without either the prior written permission of the Publishers or a licence permitting restricted copying in the United Kingdom issued by the Copyright Licensing Agency Ltd, 90 Tottenham Court Road, London WIP OLP.

Designed by Clare Sleven
Illustrations by Jonathan Adams, Jeff Edwards
Printed in Hong Kong

03 02 01 00 99
10 9 8 7 6 5 4 3 2 1

Northamptonshire Libraries & Information Service	
Peters	11-Mar-04
C932	£6.50

ISBN 0 431 00489 7
This title is also available in a hardback library edition (ISBN 0 431 00488 9).

British Library Cataloguing in Publication Data

Shuter, Jane
    Egypt : farming and food. - (Ancient world topic books)
    1 . Agriculture - Egypt - History - Juvenile literature
    2 .Egypt - History - To 332 B. C. - Juvenile literature
    I . Title
    932

Acknowledgements
The Publishers would like to thank the following for permission to reproduce photographs: British Museum: pp8, 10–11, 28, 29; Michael Holford: p16; Middle East Pictures: C Osborne p5; Photo Archiv: J Leipe pp13, 20, 21; Werner Forman Archive: pp9, 17, 23, 25

Cover photograph reproduced with permission of Jurgen Liepe, Photo-Archiv

Every effort has been made to contact copyright holders of any material reproduced in this book. Any omissions will be rectified in subsequent printings if notice is given to the Publisher.

Any words appearing in the text in bold, **like this**, are explained in the Glossary.

CONTENTS

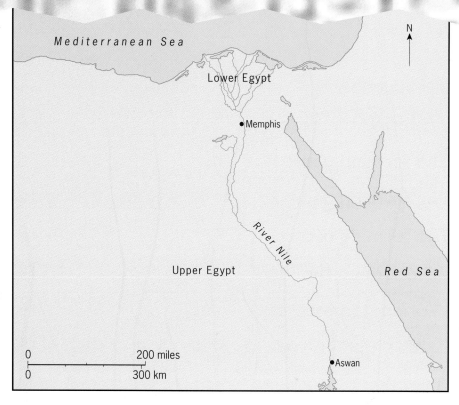

THE RIVER NILE

This chart shows different stages in the long history of Ancient Egypt. The red blocks show when **pharaohs** were weak and no one ran the whole country.

The River Nile runs the whole length of Egypt. In ancient times it flooded each year. When the water went back down, a thick layer of mud was left covering the land that had been flooded. Farmers could grow **crops** on this, but the rest of the land was too dry. They had to fit farming in around the flood (**inundation**). During the inundation they did other jobs.

Upper and Lower Egypt united 3100 BC	2566 BC Great Pyramid built	Bronze not copper used to make sharper tools	Invaders bring horses to Egypt	World's oldest map made of Egypt's gold mines		Alexander the Great takes over Egypt	Romans take over Egypt
Early Period 3100 – 2686BC	Old Kingdom 2686 – 2181BC	Middle Kingdom 2055 – 1650BC	New Kingdom 1550 – 1069BC		Late Period 747 – 332BC	Rule of Ptolemys 332 – 30BC	
3000BC	2400BC End of First Pyramid building	2nd Pyramid building period 2000BC	Shaduf now used to lift water	1000BC	Persians rule Egypt	1BC	
	2650BC First Pyramid built						

THE FARMING YEAR

There were three stages to the farming year. The inundation lasted from July to October. November to April was the planting and growing time. May to June was **harvest** time.

MEASURING THE FLOOD

It was important to know how much the river would flood each year. Walled steps were built down to the river. Marks were carved on the walls at the same time every year. (You can still see these marks today.) **Scribes** used these measures (called Nilometers) to work out how much the river was likely to flood. The river usually rose by 8–10 metres at Aswan and 6–8 metres at Memphis.

Farmers still farm along the edges of the River Nile today. Now a dam has been built to stop the yearly flooding.

WATERING THE DESERT

Most of Ancient Egypt was **desert**. It was hot and dry all year round. It hardly ever rained. Farmers had to water their **crops** every day.

For most of the Ancient Egyptian period, people lifted water from the river one bucketful at a time. Then they carried it to the fields. From earliest times, farmers tried to hold as much of the water from the **inundation** as possible.

KEEPING BACK THE WATER

Farmers made big ponds to hold the flood water. **Ditches** ran from the ponds to the fields and around them. Wooden **sluices** divided up the ditches. When the sluice boards were pulled up the water came out. When they were shut the water was held back. So farmers could let out just as much water as they needed to water their fields.

Every year people cleared weeds and mud out of the ditches and ponds before the inundation. They had to work fast. Many people helped as part of their **corvée** – work they had to do for the **pharaoh**.

As soon as the flood waters started to go down – in late October – government **scribes** measured the fields. They marked out each plot of land with stones. Then the farmers could start work. They turned over the thick mud with wooden **ploughs**, which were often pulled by **oxen**. Then the scribes gave out the **grain** to sow. They prayed to the gods for a good **harvest**. The seeds were sown and animals were driven over the soil to tread the seeds into it.

A **tomb model** of a farmer ploughing. Models like this were buried with people, along with all the other things they needed for their next life.

Farmers sowed seeds by hand, from baskets. In this picture the mud is hard. Farmers break it up before the seeds are sown.

AN EASY LIFE?

Ancient Egyptian **tomb paintings** show tomb owners farming in their best clothes. But these paintings had to show a perfect world. They wanted the dead to go to a perfect place, so this is what they showed. In real life, farming was hard work.

SOME WRITINGS FROM ANCIENT EGYPT TELL US ABOUT FARMERS. IN ABOUT 2000BC A SCRIBE WROTE:

The farmer is worn out from standing in mud, dressed in rags. By the time he has walked home at the end of the day he is exhausted. [*Some tomb paintings show farmers talking as they work. This is an example from the wall of a tomb:*] Go on, guide it! Hurry, hurry with the oxen! Mind your feet. Watch out, the master's there, and he's watching us!

In March people **harvested** the **grain**. Men, women and children flocked to the fields when the grain was ripe. It was cut down, sorted and stored. Then there was just time to grow a **crop** of beans or other vegetables before the **inundation**.

KEEPING COUNT

It was important to have enough grain to feed everyone for a whole year, so the **pharaoh**'s **scribes** organized the harvest. They worked out how much grain should come from each field. They checked how much was actually cut. Then they took a share for the pharaoh's **granaries**.

A copy of a **tomb painting** showing harvest time. The scribes are recording everything carefully.

BAD YEARS

When the River Nile had a 'low year' there was less mud left behind to grow crops in. Then there was not enough grain to feed everyone. Pharaohs had to buy grain from other countries to make sure that everyone was fed. Despite this many people died of **starvation** in bad years.

IN ABOUT 2000BC, A **PRIEST**, HEQANAKHTE, WAS SENT NORTH FROM THEBES ON BUSINESS FOR THE PHARAOH. HE WROTE TO HIS FAMILY:

Is the Nile very low this year? It seems to be here. I have collected as much food for you as I can. But it is not much, for there is not much to get. Almost everyone is looking for food.

During the **inundation** all the farm land was underwater. So farmers spent the time mending tools and looking after the animals. If they worked on land belonging to a **temple** or the **pharaoh** they were given other jobs to do. There was usually building work going on that needed lots of people to fetch and carry.

HAPY, GOD OF THE NILE

Hapy was the god who controlled the River Nile. Ancient Egyptians prayed to him for a good inundation. A low inundation could mean **starvation** for many of the poorest people. A high inundation was bad too – homes would be flooded. A low flood was feared the most as this prayer to Hapy shows (it was written in about 1800BC):

Lord of the fish, he sends the wild birds south as he rises. He is father to the barley and wheat. If he is slow to rise then people hold their breath, grow fierce as food grows short. When he rises well the people and the land rejoice.

A **tomb model** showing fishing boats.

These fishermen have already caught some fish.

The fishermen use paddles to steer and move the boats along.

The boats were made from bundles of reeds tied together.

There are tiny model fish in the net slung between the boats.

The **pharaoh** owned all the land in Ancient Egypt. But he did not run it all by himself. Most of the land was divided into **estates**. These estates were in different shapes and sizes, and were run by different people. Most of the farmers worked on the estates.

ESTATES

The biggest estates gave everything they made or grew to the pharaoh or important **temples**. The pharaoh's lands were run by important families who often had smaller estates of their own. They kept most of the **crops** from their estates (they had to give some to the pharaoh as a **tax**). They passed their estates on to their children. But the pharaoh could take their estates away from them at any time. He could also take the **grain** from their **granaries** to feed people when grain was scarce.

An Ancient Egyptian estate. The family that ran the estate would have lived in the large central building, surrounded by storerooms and rooms for the servants.

Historians today are not sure if Ancient Egyptian farmers rented the land they farmed. They may have farmed the land in return for a home and part of the **crops**. We do know that they all worked on **estates**, although some farmers seem to have taken on extra land to farm for themselves.

A PIECE OF LAND

Farming land was divided up into pieces called **aruras**. Each arura grew enough food to feed a family for a year. Most farmers farmed one arura for the estate. Some families farmed spare land for themselves. The crops from any extra land they farmed were theirs to keep or sell after they had given up part of it as **tax**.

Farmers had only wooden tools to work with for most of the Ancient Egyptian period.

handplough

These scoops were used to shake off the outside layer of the **grain**.

FLOOD TIME

We do not know exactly what all farmers did during the **inundation**. Workers on big estates owned by **temples** or the **pharaoh** did building work for their masters. Many farmers on smaller estates did other work on the estate. Some farmers may have had a second job, such as basket-making, which they did at this time.

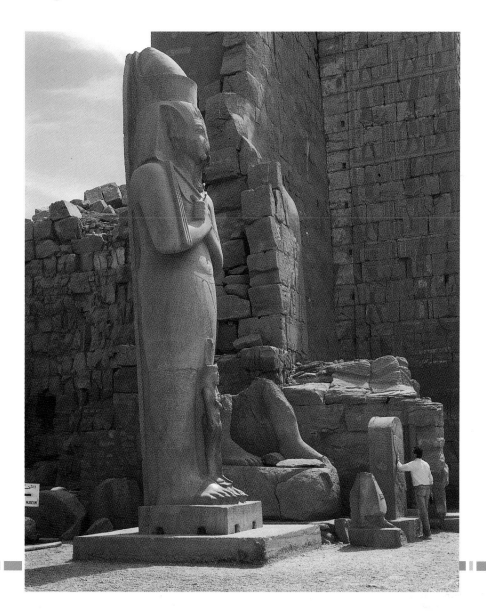

The Ancient Egyptians had no machinery and very few labour-saving tools. So all building jobs needed lots of people to move huge stones or sculptures, like the one in the picture, to the right places. During the inundation, this provided work for the farmers.

The most important food and drink in Ancient Egypt were bread and beer. Both were made from **grain** – barley or emmer (a type of wheat). So it was important to grow a lot of grain and store it carefully.

BREAD

There were many types of bread of different shapes and made with flour from different mixes of grain. The flour was made by crushing the grain and shaking off the outside **husks**. The grain was then **ground** between two stones. The flour had bits of stone in it, which came from the grinding. So the bread was gritty and wore away the Egyptians' teeth! The flour was mixed with water and baked in ovens.

BEER

Beer was made from partly-baked barley bread, barley and water. This was all mashed up together, left for a few days and then strained into beer jars. It was still thick and lumpy and had to be drunk through a wooden strainer (like a thick straw)!

A closer view of a **granary**. You can see the different bins for the different sorts of grain. Servants are collecting grain, and it is being measured out and recorded. Others are husking and grinding corn.

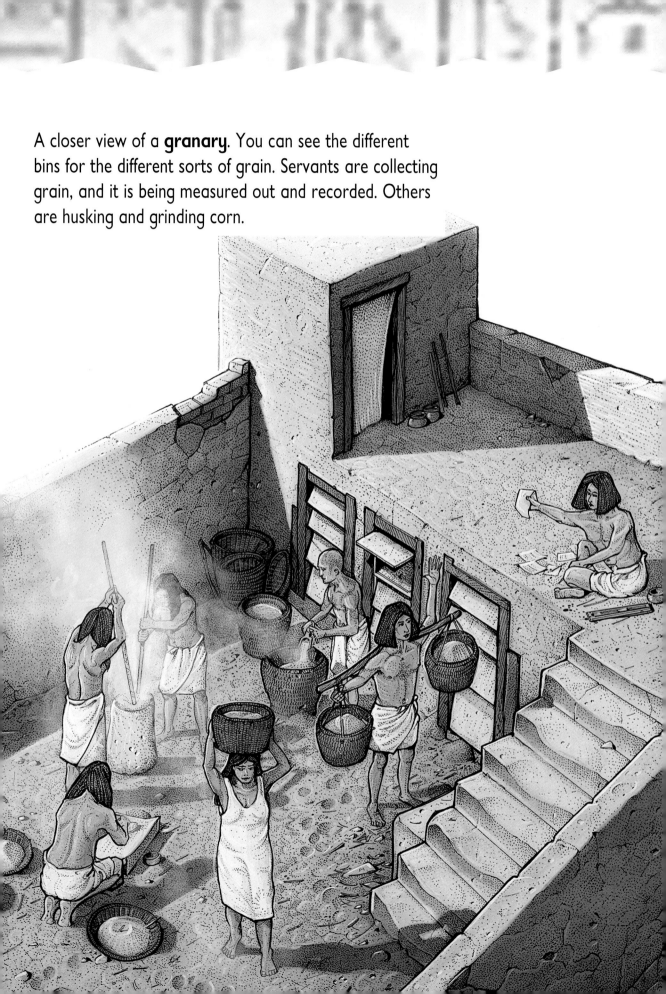

ANIMALS

Owning animals was a sign of wealth in Ancient Egypt. Animals were also killed in **religious ceremonies** for the gods. There were ordinary uses for animals, too.

Cattle were used to pull the **ploughs**. But most animals were raised as food. Cows, sheep and goats were kept for milk and meat. Animal skins were used for clothes and sandals. Ducks and geese were kept for eggs and meat. Fish were often kept in the duck ponds. Bees were kept in hives for honey to sweeten food and drink.

This model is from the **tomb** of an important Egyptian, Chancellor Meketre. It shows Meketre watching his cattle being counted.

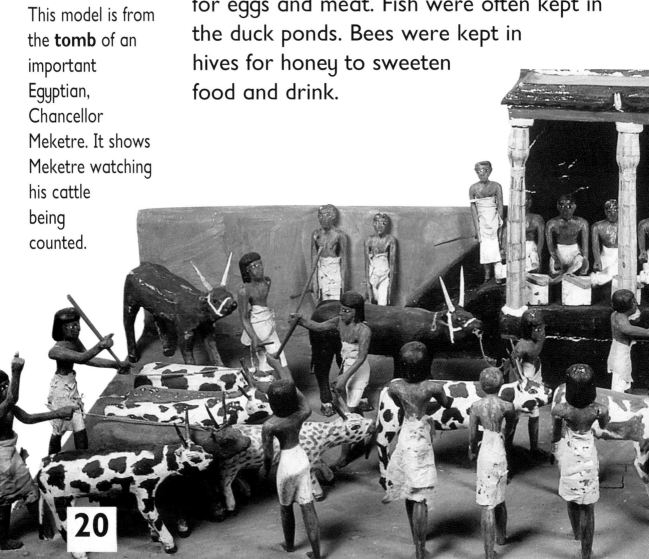

COUNTING UP

Every year or two, all the animals on an **estate** were caught and counted – not just the cows and goats, but the ducks and geese as well. The owner of the estate sat and watched as all the animals were driven past. The work could take days.

Scribes wrote down how many animals there were. **Herdsmen** who had looked after their animals well were rewarded. Those who had not were punished. Then the animals were divided up: some were kept and some were killed.

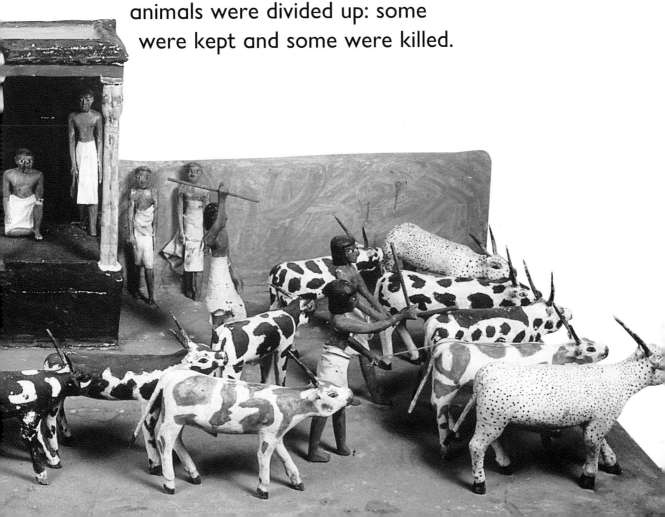

HUNTING FOR FOOD

The Ancient Egyptians hunted birds and fish on the river for food. Fishermen made a living catching fish. Some people made a living hunting wild birds for rich people to eat. Rich people went hunting for fun, when they felt like it. **Tomb paintings** show the river and marshes full of birds and fish. Tomb paintings had to show life as being perfect so that the dead person's **afterlife** was perfect too!

THIS POEM, FROM ABOUT 2000BC, DESCRIBES A DAY'S HUNTING.

We go down to the marsh, to trap birds and catch fish. It is a happy day, the marsh goddess is good to us. I make a screen for myself from the sun and settle on the riverbank. There are so many fish that my spear for catching them is never still. We get our bird nets ready. We pull the ropes when we hear them quack on the lake.

Wild birds were caught in a net and then prepared for cooking or storing.

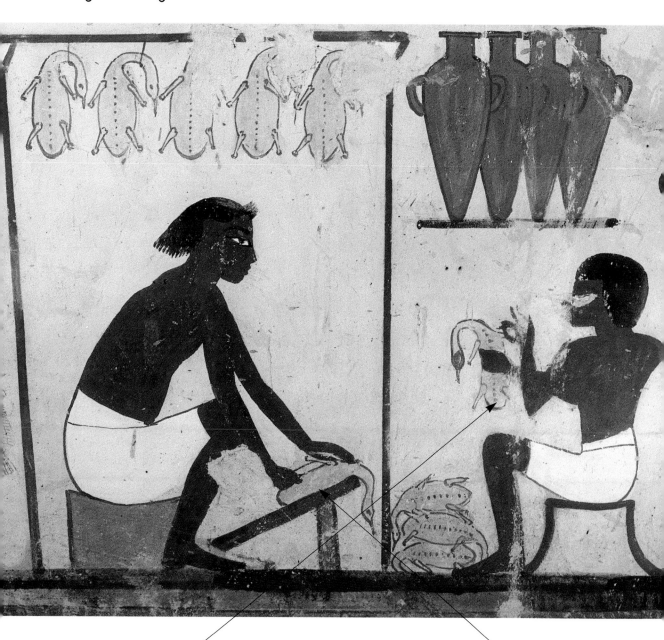

The feathers were plucked off the ducks while they were still warm.

The plucked ducks then had their insides taken out and were hung in the sun to dry.

OTHER FOODS

VEGETABLES

Most ordinary Ancient Egyptians could not very often afford to buy meat or fish to eat. They lived mostly on bread, beer and vegetables. They grew many different vegetables, including onions, leeks, cabbages, lettuce, cucumbers and different sorts of beans.

VEGETABLES AND HERBS WERE MORE THAN JUST FOODS. THEY WERE USED BY DOCTORS AS MEDICINE. THIS IS PART OF A BOOK OF MEDICAL CURES, WRITTEN IN ABOUT 1500BC. THE EGYPTIANS BELIEVED THAT MANY ILLNESSES WERE CAUSED BY BLOOD AND OTHER LIQUIDS GETTING BLOCKED IN THE BODY.

If there is a blockage in the arm you must give the patient fish and beer until he vomits. This clears the blockage. Then bandage his fingers with melon.

If the bowel is blocked, give the patient four pills made by mixing cucumber, senna and sycamore seeds to a paste.

Grapes were eaten as fruit and made into wine. Here, workers are picking grapes and treading them to make juice. The juice was collected as it came out of the spout on the right. It was then strained into wine jars.

FRUIT

The Egyptians planted fruit trees in gardens and along paths and rivers, as well as in orchards. Dates, figs, pomegranates and grapes all grew well in the hot weather.

ORDINARY MEALS

Most cooking was done outside. Ovens were built in the yards of houses, where the **grain** was stored. Bread was cooked in the ovens. Most other foods were cooked over an open fire. Ordinary people often cooked and ate their meals on the roofs of their houses, protected from the sun by a linen sheet on poles. People ate their main meal in the cool of the evening. They ate bread, vegetables, cheese and fruit. They ate salted and fresh fish, but not much meat. They drank beer or milk.

FEASTING

Rich people often ate in the garden. They ate the same things as ordinary people, but had meat more often and drank wine as well as beer. **Feast** times were different. It was important to have lots to eat and drink. People ate vegetables cooked in different ways. They ate beef, goat, lamb and all sorts of birds. On very special days they might eat unusual meats, like ostrich or giraffe.

A feast in an important home. The servants serve the food. The guests eat, listen to music and watch the dancers.

HOW DO WE KNOW WHAT THEY ATE?

EVIDENCE FROM THE TIME

We know what food the Ancient Egyptians ate because some **tomb paintings** show people eating or growing foods. **Tomb models** also show people cooking. We even have food from the time which has been preserved in tombs.

GROWING FOOD

Tomb paintings and models show us how Egyptian farmers grew food. Some farming tools have survived, too. The tools were made from wood. Egyptian farmers use similar methods today, although their tools are more modern.

This food was left for the dead in a tomb. There is bread, chicken, salt fish and fruit.

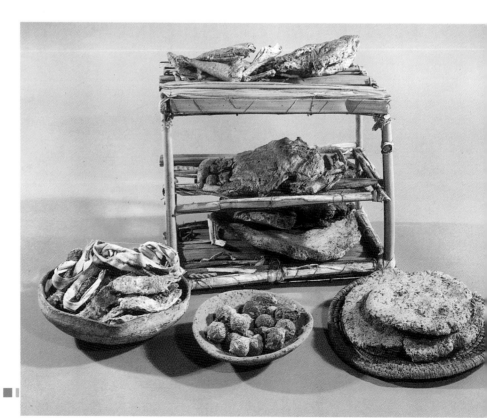

NEW EVIDENCE

Archaeologists have studied the food from Ancient Egypt. They have studied the bodies of Ancient Egyptians. This has told them about the food these people ate. They found stone grit and sand in the bread, and realized that this explained why Ancient Egyptians' teeth were so worn down.

This tomb painting shows the pond in the garden of a rich Egyptian. The pond is full of fish. Trees grow around the edges.

NEW MEDICINE?

A study of the ways herbs and foods were used in medicine shows that some Ancient Egyptian herbal cures are very like cures used today.

- Senna is still used to clear out people's bowels.
- The Ancient Egyptians chewed willow leaves to stop pain. Scientists have studied willow leaves and found that they make a chemical very like that in aspirin (which is used today to stop pain).

afterlife the place where the Ancient Egyptians believed the dead lived

archaeologists people who dig up and study things left behind from past times

arura a piece of land that was big enough to grow enough food to feed a family for a year (about three-quarters of an acre)

corvée all Ancient Egyptians who were not scribes had to do this work on the pharaoh's land for a set number of days each year

crops plants that farmers grow for food or to use in other ways (to make clothes, baskets or paper)

desert a dry place which has little or no rain all year

ditch a ditch is long and narrow, and dug out around a piece of land to trap water draining off it or to take water to it

estate a large piece of land with homes and farm land, all run by the same person

feast a special meal with lots of different things to eat and drink. Feasts often celebrate special days.

grain types of grasses with fat seeds which are eaten. Barley, wheat, rye, oats and rice are all grains.

granaries special places where grain is stored to keep it dry and to keep wild animals, such as mice, from eating it

ground crushing grain up until it is a powder (flour) and not seeds any more

harvest to cut down, collect up and store crops that are ready to eat

herdsmen people who look after lots of animals that are kept all together

husk the outside skin of a single piece of grain

inundation the time when the River Nile flooded and all the fields were underwater

mummies bodies of dead people that had been preserved

oxen a type of cattle (cows and bulls)

pharaoh the king who ruled Egypt

plough a tool that turns over the soil to break it up

religious ceremonies special times when people go to one place to pray to a god or goddess

scribes the only people in Ancient Egypt who could read and write. Scribes ran the country for the pharaoh.

sluice a board across a ditch that can be lifted or shut to let water out or hold it in

starvation not having enough to eat

tax a payment that you have to make to whoever is running the country

temple a place where gods and goddesses are worshipped

tomb a place where someone is buried

tomb models tiny carvings or pottery shapes of people and things that were put in tombs

tomb paintings paintings on the walls of tombs